S0-BND-933

ACKNOWLEDGEMENTS

Some of these poems first appeared in: Cyphers, Gown
Literary Supplement, Honest Ulsterman, The Belfast
Newsletter. Poetry Ireland Review, Poetry Review, The
Rialto, Seneca Review (USA), Southern Review (USA),
Stand, Windows Selection. Rosguill was read on
All Arts and Parts (Radio Ulster).

Lapwing Publications gratefully acknowledge
the financial assistance of the **Arts Council of
Northern Ireland** and **The UK Foundation for
Sport and the Arts** in the publication of this
pamphlet.

3

CHICAGO PUBLIC LIBRARY
BEVERLY BRANCH
1962 W. 95th STREET
CHICAGO, IL   60643

4

DISCARD

MADONNA
OF THE SPACES

JANET SHEPPERSON

CHICAGO PUBLIC LIBRARY
BEVERLY BRANCH
1962 W. 95th STREET
CHICAGO, IL   60643

1

PUBLISHED BY
LAPWING PUBLICATIONS
c/o DENNIS & RENE GREIG
1 BALLYSILLAN DRIVE
BELFAST BT14 8HQ

TYPESET BY
LAPWING GRAFIX
c/o BRIAN CHRISTIE
51 KILCOOLE GDNS
TELE: 712483

PRINTED BY TEXTFLOW SERVICES LTD
SCIENCE LIBRARY, MALONE ROAD BELFAST
TEL: 663591

ISBN 1 898472 00 9

LAPWING POETRY PAMPHLET
Janet Shepperson: Madonna of the Spaces
PUBLISHED 1993
COPYRIGHT REMAINS WITH AUTHOR

CONTENTS

FEMALE NUDE

From where she lies, she can just see the edge of
  the window.
She's watched the swifts lacing the sky with black
  threads,
travelling South and returning so many times
in the time it has taken him to re-arrange
her body: compliant limbs spreading and rippling
in a square of light that gives her flesh the
  sheen
of an over-ripe peach, gold, with a bloom of dust.
He's been gone ages now. The smell of turps,
oil paint, the smoke from his pipe, disperse in the
  draught
from the rattling window. She lumbers to her feet,
stiff, after lying still for centuries.

The thing won't close.
Down in the street,
running, hustling,
a crowd of women -
thin and tense.
Greyhounds. Gazelles.
We can do it
stamped on their T shirts.

Working, sweating,
honing their flesh,
their gleaming limbs
jerk as if pulled
by invisible strings.
The ad man's dream -
the puppet master?
She strains at the window.

Still it won't close and their high-pitched voices
    reach her
- bossy, nervy creatures in love with movement.
She cannot join them, all she can do is imagine
him with his tired frown, sighing, throwing a
    cloth
over the easel, knotting the puppet strings
to the bars of the window, but loosely, so that
    they slip
little by little into the street below.

PRIVATE VIEWING

She's a small person loitering nervously
in the corner of a warehouse full of paintings.
They're paintings of the gaps between things.
She crouches in the gaps and hates the paintings
because they're all about the way each time
she opens her mouth it comes out wrong and people
listen but their arms are folded against her,
their bodies are saying *Is that the time? I must go.*

She's a single woman menaced by the cosy
grumpiness of marriages, by the dazzle
of radical feminists in huge shiny earrings
and by herself in the mirror at seven a.m.
saying *Your hair is all wrong and there's a*
*   muscle*
at the corner of your mouth that won't stop
*   twitching*
and you embarrassed me yesterday, creeping about
avoiding people's eyes at the private viewing.

Up a dusty staircase in the warehouse
is the part they ignored when they made it into a
    gallery:
a small room full of scaffolding left by the
    builders
and torn out plumbing and rusty pipes and
    railings -
It reminds her of the heap of old scrap metal
squatting on the dockside, where the wind
whistles through the gaps and sometimes kids
climb precariously up the twisted rungs.

She thinks she'd like to take it to work with her,
and tether it to her desk - mentally adding
some buckled pram wheels, claws from a JCB,
the guts and entrails of a burnt-out bus,
the skeleton of a scooter she had as a child.
But where it would be most at home is in
the warehouse, downstairs at the viewing,
    labelled
Installation With Gaps And Small Person,

surrounded by people sipping wine, assessing
the work's importance and each other's reactions,
and she'd be a pair of eyes in the midst of the
    heap,
peering out at the drinkers through the gaps.

DANCING ON ICE (1963)

Come in, girls. Playtime's over. Kennedy's been
   shot.
The world is holding its breath. We're watching
   history
being made on a tiny black-and-white screen we've
   wheeled
into the gym (where it's warm). Now, girls,
   come in.

   We're out here on the ice,
   polishing up our slides,
   our breath is steam in the air,
   our feet are slipping sideways,
   circling to a new song
   for slides: *Let's twist again,*
   Like we did last summer ...

Come in, girls. Summer's over. The newspapers
   have pictures
of Lee Harvey Oswald - they say he was a Marxist -
they say the fear of communists in America could
   grow
into a red nightmare, raise tensions in Berlin
and many other cities - in this divided world -

In this divided world
boys sit one side of the hall,
girls sit the other, and wait
to be asked up. Not us.
We don't need boys to help us
wriggle and slither and scream
and swoop across the ice -

Come in, girls. Ice is dangerous. And a woman is
   still a woman.
Every girl should have a career for a while -
   until she marries.
Even that space woman, Valentina Tereshkova,
has married an astronaut: the world's first space
   couple.

Who's going to wash the dishes
when they get home from space?

Well, she is, I suppose. But that's hardly the
   point.
A woman needs a man, she needs a shoulder to lean
   on.
Think of the fun your mothers had in the Forties:
   nightingales
singing in Berkeley Square, his arm around her
   waist,
protectively. Her white-gloved hand flirting in
   his...

We need our hands free
for balance, learning the steps
of a dance that has no steps.
Our heads don't know what's happening
but we're thinking with our feet ...

Do you want to be left out, facing middle age
with no partner at all? For the last time girls,
    come in.

No more wallflowers,
no one two three, one
two three, in the gym, waiting
to be swept off our feet by *him*.
For the first time dancing apart,
heartscared and proud,
out here, on our own
two feet. We won't come in.

PAVEMENT

The paving stones become huge fields, divided
by ditches, as the child teeters across
in her mother's high-heeled shoes. Her tiny feet
slop from side to side; one shoe capsizes
and pulls her down outside the greengrocer's,
trays of fruit cascading round her, oranges
scuttling into the gutter, each a world
rolling out of her reach, dimpled and ridged
with puddles, hillsides, clumps of yellow grass.

Inside her head, her mother scolds. Slowly
the bright globes diminish to background.
   The child
hobbles painfully homewards in the shoes:
a half-tame pony, tethered to a threadbare
shrinking verge, by these beautiful useless
   symbols.

A DIFFERENT FATHER

Friday. Kept in again,
avoiding my eye and the page,
he's written 10th March, his name,
and made thirty holes in the floor
with a pair of compasses.

The others are romping home:
his sleek brothers and sisters,
fast workers, tossing
their schoolbags over the hedge.
He stays in his corner -

a twilight cave where he crouches
shaggy and bloated, among
chewed pencils, dismembered bones,
ignores passing dinosaurs.
It's not that he's stupid,

his mother asserts. *He just*
won't work. It all runs off him
like water off a duck's back.
He had a different father
from the others, you know.

Yes. The others are high
fliers, and he is grounded
like a moulting drake in a pond.
We throw crusts of information.
He picks them up, drops them.

Head mostly under his wing.
Our feeble scoldings muffled
by raggedy feathers. Warm
close-to-the-body darkness.
He gazes into it,

blinks, tries to make out
a fading image: a big
man with a slow smile
hoisting his tiny son
on to solid shoulders.

THE WRONG COLOUR

A litter of stones harassing our feet
as we labour up to the viewing point -
rocks turning slippery, tilting,
screes opening, dragging us backwards.

So it seems entirely logical
when you start to describe the recently
approved plan: *Get rid of the rocks.*
Useless things messing up the landscape

and always the wrong colour - not
the cold clear grey the tourists expect
but a sulky brown, as if they've festered
for years under stagnant water and mud.

I remember days in the high mountains;
ferns and stonecrop in crevices,
thyme and saxifrage spilling over
outcrops the colour of winter dusk.

But here it is never dusk. The light
is always the same. Nothing can grow
on these odd-coloured barren lumps.
My throat is choked, I can't speak

to warn you: if you clear the slopes,
they'll fold in on themselves like soft
flesh without bones, collapsing, sinking,
treacherous as scum on a bog

until the last rock drags the sky
down to clench and knot around it
so that the rain comes. Then all colours
will be the same, and blotted out.

AFTER THE MARRIAGE

(1)

It sparkled like a white Venetian palace,
trefoils and curves, a wedding cake of stone
iced with new rainbows. They were never selfish,
they wouldn't keep it for themselves alone;
they opened it to students and to tourists
and lost ones looking for a place to stay.
Wave-nibbled stilts raised it above the water
that smelt of green and August and decay.
Right from the first it needed scaffolding,
it couldn't stand the weight they made it bear,
and after years of worry and expense
they found the fragile stones beyond repair,
and watched the gleam of their brave fantasy
crumble, and touch the greyness of the sea.

(2)

His single bed creaks though there's no-one in it.
The fan hums all night in his hotel room.
He shakes his fingers, coughs, to clear the sticky
membranes clinging round him like a womb.
This is what's left of all they'd built: the slimy
trails in the water, stumps of rotting wood;
she dips her oars in grey and green, the subtle
colours of sea he never understood
and pulls away. Her boat spins in the current,
always dragged back. He feels her sea-sickness
from far away, churning in his own stomach
as he moves inland, sees her drowning face
in every paving stone. The streets are bare.
The light becomes the colour of her hair.

(3)

That was when you started to look for me.
Thought I'd be cold, you said; you still couldn't
    grasp
my need to be always out-of-season, moving
in random circles, sifting through the past
at the expense of the future, feeling the chill
currents sweep me past each landing stage.
That was my freedom; yours was walking slowly
past the lighted windows of each cage
calling them *houses*, trying to get inside.
But space grew wider round you however close
to the warmth you tried to get. And space
    clenched in
round me, confined me, thickened to enclose
my solitude, my fear that I would choke
on fear - my own, or yours. The pattern broke

(4)

when I caught you by the arm, crying *Leave me alone*.
We found ourselves in an empty echoing square
with a winter feel to it, all the cafes shuttered,
a litter of closed-up parasols and chairs
lapping the edges of buildings like a tide -
but you had given up on buildings; I
had given up on water. Pigeon's wings
fretted, scribbled, smudged the darkening sky,
writhing and settling like snowflakes, grey on grey.
White is a lie, you said. *A trick of the light.*
Can't last. And *Neither can movement*, I said.
My fingers froze in yours. Only the slight
nudge of your pulse disturbed me, offering
the rhythm of the tide beneath your skin.

THE SCRATCH

Flaunting their richness of age, their
   almost-perfection,
the Persian rugs glow with their stained-glass
   colours:
amber, russet, crimson, faultless crescents,
arches, flights of steps, all delicately
balanced: one deliberate black knot spoiling
the symmetry. "Allah alone is perfect."

Even the early settlers in New England
gathered their patient triangles of patchwork
into a flourish of little horses ramping
across striped winter fields - but sewed wrong
   colours
into the final row, fearing to challenge
the powerful, obtuse God they imagined.

You have no such Gods.
No need to fear achieving
perfection. What you give
me is spoiled already:
a tiny marble box,
its careful lustrous curves
intricately patterned -
a jagged white mark
scored across their smoothness.

I lick my finger and rub;
the scratch dissolves like salt.
The wetness dries; the scratch
re-makes itself, rough-edged,
permanent as a scar.

If I gaze long enough, I can see the whole pattern
    move -
crawling with moss and sand and rust and silver
melting into each other, under the thin
streak that is like the single slash of white
where bark has been torn from a tree trunk,
    opening
up the whole forest, drawing the eye on into
deep shadows where the movement of every leaf
creates new colours I've never seen before.

CHEVAUX-DE-FRISE

Some people's defences are an art form.
Yours are more physical. You've backed away
till your retreat is cut off by the sea
and what you can't ignore becomes a storm

battering this promontory. It provides
a chance for us to discuss the weather, as if
it's Out There, not inside us. Then a brief
lull in the storm, at dusk, the wind subsides

and leaves me sitting on the landward side
in front of all these stones forbiddingly
stuck in the ground like stakes for the cavalry
to stumble over. But they've had their last ride

and my pain is lessened because I've found the name
for the spiky stones in some book: *chevaux-de-frise.*
I stare at the sea and wonder how long this truce
will have to last, before the urge to blame

is forgotten, and you lurch to your feet,
    thirst-crazed,
concentrating hard as you thread your way,
cursing, bruising your shins, breathing heavily,
out through the stubborn remnants of this maze.

SYNCHRONIZING

Two single sleeping bags:
husks of our former lives,
smelling of heather, grass
curled in unvisited corners -

even here in the dark they are fading,
shrivelling, wearing away
to nothing, ready to split
as the skin of a crysalis

bursts, and a clutched dampness
of daylight heaves itself out
and opens into wings
that shimmer and pulse with light.

This is where we sleep
now, in a fan of soft
colours that ripple and spread
around us all night long

and even in sleep we adjust
our bodies to perfect balance,
synchronizing our breath
so that neither wing will drag

on the other, send the whole
thing tilting and careering
lopsidedly towards
winter, or wherever

we left those narrow husks
of our old, clenched-in selves
each lying alone, staring
into the creaking dark.

LOSING COUNT

I watch the miles unravel,
strung with beads of brightness
flicking through the sea mist:

seventeen - a sail,
a leaping dolphin's back,
somewhere close inshore,

twenty - gannets diving,
fulmars chuckling on ledges
along the basalt cliffs,

forty - a waterfall
plunging through the bracken
sheer into the sea,

fifty - crumpled rock
scattered round our wheels,
and the road ebbing inland

to tally with names from the guide book:
The Blue Glen, Field of the Bramble,
Hill of the Two Winds.

Somewhere we must have crossed
the Ford of the Stranger. Numbers
are sliding off the dashboard

losing their digital clarity,
furring up like the bodies
of moths smashed on the windscreen.

It's time to leave the car
and go on foot. The sky
heaving itself from the fog

is unexpected, luminous,
glazed with afterblue,
the mountains ripening,

the sun at our backs dissolving
distances, drawing horizons
of tawny and gold towards us.

CHILDLESS

Slinky, screeching, dark, they skite about
like swifts in next door's garden, following
their flightpaths through an airspace that can turn
solid for them to slide on, hang from, swing -

or wanting the sound of the waves, they redesign
their strip of grass and bushes as an island,
they prance into the spray and scurry back,
bedraggled, damp, to catch hold of her hand -

"Mummy, he says I'm ugly." "He says I'm a girn."
"Well then don't play with him. There's other fish
in the sea." The kitchen window is a lighthouse,
from far out in their boat they see it flash

as they tack unsteadily across the garden,
then the real rain starts. I hear her call them in.
I watch the walls of their house bulge and turn
   liquid
with laughter, till the rooms rock up and down -

Our house is childless. Rooms have never
   stretched
nor walls dissolved. These mornings we sleep long
in a bed engulfed by sand. Each month we carve
fantastic shapes and wait for the tide's tongue

to snake up the moat and lick the sides till they
   crumble
under the sea's huge swirling swishing run,
hemming us in and dragging us out and crowding us
to the edges of our lives. But it never comes.

Because of the sea's absence we hear the wind
louder and louder all night, becoming the voice
of absence itself, commenting on the dull
parade of space after space after space after
   space.

GHOST TRAIN

(1)
After the first X-ray,
the doctor demonstrates:
These (crooking his arms)
are your fallopian tubes
and these (flexing his fingers)
are fimbria. This is where
(if your tubes were open)
the dye would come oozing out ...

I dream of the hospital:
the darkened ward contracts,
becomes my womb, with me
scrabbling at walls to find
openings, passages - dragged
into a childhood memory
- the ghost train slithering
through tunnels dimly lit
by the faint luminous seepage
of blue dye - feathery
fingers brushing my face -
gone before I can catch them -
scarlet letters flashing
on doors, forming words
in an unknown alphabet -
just as it starts to make sense,
a man in a white coat
flicks a switch. The words
shiver, distort, dissolve
and every door I come to
is smooth and black and closed.

(2)

.Even the anaesthetist
can't find my veins. They shrink
at the first touch of the needle,
retreating like a snail's
antennae, into a shell
of deceptively docile flesh
and the sensible voice in my head
- *For your own good* - fails
to draw them out again.

When I finally go under,
I dream I'm giving birth:
Push, they say, and I push.
Out come streams of sparks
hissing and spitting, then
scarlet tongues of flame
sliding from sheet to floor
- these are my veins, crackling
coiling seething jumping,
intent on their spectral dance
of blood and flickering light.

ROSGUILL

Year after year I return to this windblown country
of perfect miniatures: the cottage crouching
in the lee of a hill, its windows blurred with
   salt,
its hearth overgrown by forests of jackdaws'
   leavings
from a chimney-nest: slivers of turf, sheep's wool,
cracked fuchsia twigs. Outside, the wheatears
flick from stone to stone of the ruined wall,
the cock reflecting all the shoreline colours:
grey for the water; white - the rake of foam
along the high tide line of black seaweed;
pale tawny gold - the flawless crescent of beach
basking on itself, smooth as new skin.

But not this year. This year the rocks have come -
as if they had been scattered there - or grown
raggedly out of the sand, stubbly black
things gulping for air. I have to nerve
myself to walk straight past and not look back
to see if they're following. I think of night
camouflaging them as they rattle together
like some starved animal's skeleton, growing new
   fur,
lumbering into the water to be swept
out past the headland, into infinity.

Still every morning finds them on the shore
in their familiar shape, glazed with blown spray,
knowing nothing can shift them, not even the wind
that scours with sand the whole peninsula,
burying villages down the centuries,
nudging the dunes and lifting them to lay bare
earth's old tired bones.

RECLAIMED LAND

The end of the line. Rust
flakes from the tangled tracks
skewed across a barren
spit of scrawny shingle.

I search for plovers' eggs,
freckled among the stones;
find only the wind, scraping
the endless greyness, battering

abandoned goods trucks.
Shelter. The rotting planks
disclose a tentative circle
of green, edging outwards:

gorse, bramble, some tiny
tenacious saltproof plant
with feathery leaves, asserting
the survival of small things.

Warmed by a moment's sunshine,
a white butterfly
pauses among the nettles.
A twist of silver paper

and the ring-pull from a can
I take as evidence
that other survivors passed
this way, and will again.

WATCHING THE PARADE AT LARNACA

Along the Palm Tree Promenade, four deep,
they line the route and wave heart-shaped balloons
as the procession moves sedately past
Theo's Bar, the Dolphin Restaurant:
silver trumpets glitter, scarlet banners
sway with tassels, lanterns, filigree,
meek sailors in white hats and solemn girls
in white gloves guide a huge beribboned cross,
decked out with flowers, under lines of flags:
Greece is blue and white, Cyprus is gold -
an undivided island - with green leaves.

No matter that it hasn't rained for months
and nothing is green and UN soldiers pace
up and down barbed wire in Nicosia
and the woman with what seems to be a gold
chain of office, beaming, keeping step
with the Patriarch in his lush embroidered robes
may turn out to be only the President's wife.

No matter. In this handful of photographs
taken from a hotel balcony
it's always the moment after a day of rain
when every face in the crowd is turned towards
her smile - relaxed and easy - genuine;
no-one has eyes for the Patriarch; the sun
has just come out in time to show her shadow,
regal, an inch or two ahead of his.

ICONOSTASIS

Crammed with icons, sagging under
the weight of saints and heroes frozen
in the act of dragon-spearing, or
brandishing books or unexplained arrows.
Eagles peer down. Pelicans.
Byzantine shades to baroque: a Virgin
with clouds and cherubs, sheeted in plastic,
kissed by the faithful. Gilded by love
and money, wreathed in pineapple leaves,
fish scales and feathers up to the ceiling.

I feel them pushing me back. They're meant to.
Only the priests - all men - may enter
the sanctuary. A velvet curtain
fills the doorway, keeps at bay
the horned gods, the goddesses -
Athena, Artemis, Aphrodite.
I twitch the curtain aside: a clock
(modern), dusters, cleaning fluid.
From a hook on the whitewashed wall
the priest's black robes hang like bats' wings.

CHURCH OF THE ARCHANGEL MICHAEL

Among the olive trees, the small dome broods
like an outdoor oven: walls the colour of bread:
no windows. Doors thrown open once a year
on Michael's feast day: no electric lights,
no gold iconostasis topped with dragons,
with lamps that swing on chains from gilded snouts:

just close, earthy darkness.
A woman dressed in black
lighting matches, pointing:
figures on the walls.
"This - Mary and Jesus.
This - John the Baptist.
This - Saint Helena.
This - Saint Lazarus."
Hands uplifted, haloes,
wings, solemn eyes
staring down until
she runs out of matches,
out of English words.

Eight centuries of damp and candle smoke
have tarnished the bright robes, nibbled the feet,
cobwebbed the heads that bend to us, benign
or ominous, then fade, retreat to where
they've always been: the dark behind our eyes.

APHRODITE'S SABBATICAL

Aphrodite, electing to travel West,
tired of Orthodox churches with their stifled
mournful-eyed tight-haloed iconed women,
made a foray into the Protestant churches -

Frankfurt, Geneva, Glasgow, Belfast. *Dour*
was a word she thought of then abandoned. These
were airy places where the daylight tapped
continuously on gleaming window panes.

She peered over the tops of box pews,
scanned altar and pulpit for local images;
she found no women trapped in icons here -
She found no women. She heard the preacher insist

Nothing must be allowed to stand in the way
of our relationship with God. We want
no graven images. We want the Word
of God, and only the Word. We want it spelt out.

She searched for the Word and found it on a
    pedestal
upheld by a brass eagle. A cold eye
and claws and a beak presented today's text:
The Letter killeth, the Spirit giveth life.

She concluded her survey with a couple of sightings
of the Holy Spirit fluttering about
among the hymn books and the tablets of stone,
looking worried and inarticulate.

THE APHRODITE STONE

The stone is what I've salvaged
from winter-bruised Akamas, the limestone cliffs
that curl into caves and grottoes, crumble
into a wave-locked Burren where thistle and thorn
nuzzle apart the vertebrae of rock
and the tide is all the music
of pebbles grinding churning abrading hammering
holes in each other.

The stone is a sculpture
by Henry Moore, with a gap hollowed out
where the heart and guts should be.

The stone is a woman
crouched on the edge of the bed - she cradles
her breasts that still hang heavy, blindly seeking
tiny mouths to suck, refusing to be
comforted, refusing to know
that the child was never a child but a clot of
   blood
ebbing out of her
leaving a cavity
for the wind to whistle through.

The stone is a souvenir
from Aphrodite's birthplace from the rock
where she perched like a mermaid posing for the
   tourists
till her honey-coloured flesh faded to grey
weathered fractured fissured pock-marked pocketed
into holes and then worn smooth
by the undertow,
abandoned
above high water mark.

The stone says: Hold me
in the hollow of your hand.

MADONNA OF THE SPACES

Botticelli might have painted
her thoughtful tawny eyes
and capable sunburnt hands
in her lap, cradling nothing;

after several botched attempts,
the baby's chubby limbs
and petulant sleepy face
have finally been erased,

leaving an aureole -
faint gold flecks of dust
fading to a halo-shaped
dent in the canvas

through which the weather pushes
its tangled, damp threads -
a promise of water flicking
in and out of willows,

playing with the reflections
of women who kneel at the edge
to wash clothes and gossip
into the blue distance.

This is what she sees -
figures trudging up crazy
goat paths to the walled
city. Market day.

Shoulders braced to the weight
of baskets. Through the mesh
something shining - fish,
olives, damsons, grapes?

She stretches, flexing her wrists,
wanting to follow but held
back by the suspicion
that they've been trying to harvest

the sparkle of light from the river,
stuffing it into their panniers
and it pouring out as fast,
tumbling down the rocks,

leaving a silver trail,
till every basket holds
simply the shape of itself
sculptured in emptiness.

THIS ROOM IS CLOSING NOW

Here, under glass, a flourish of stems and leaves
transfixed by a typed label: English or Irish,
Fifteenth or Sixteenth Century. Every stitch
as bright as if it had ripened just this morning

Under her careful needle. We gaze and gaze
as if her whole life's preserved behind glass:
   perhaps
it was: English or Irish, sitting for years
with her back to the fire, her face to the
   flickering window

whose small crabbed panes would hide and reveal
   the shapes
of what might be horses grazing, or the wind
caught in the blackthorn bushes, or crouched
   figures
in the dusk, surrounding the tower. But at her
   feet

the wolfhounds slept on undisturbed, their coats
tangled with the silks that spilled from her
   clawed
arthritic hands, as she rested between births,
her crippled body too stiff for the narrow stairs,

she worked while daylight lasted, and when the sun
touched the marsh to gold, she thought of fire
in the thatch, wood smouldering, flaring up, the
   glass
splintering and slivers of it seeming

to lodge in her gut where the pain twisted and
   deepened
and the bleeding would not stop. Day after day
it was draining out of her, soft and dark and cold
as the damp that seeped through the tapestry from
   the stones,

yet still her needle laboured to create
herself pacing among the clipped yew hedges,
her hand on the collar of some heraldic beast
in a garden of herbs, St. John's wort, rosemary,

chamomile, comfrey, simples for every ill,
fruits without blemish, flowers of burnished gold
and the baby curled inside her, static and proud
as the shining curves of the phoenix in the tree -

or so it seems to us, as the attendant
covers the glass - "This room is closing now" -
and we make for the exit, a wet October night,
the swish of tyres, the street lights going on.